ST. AUGUSTINE IN 90 MINUTES

St. Augustine
IN 90 MINUTES

Paul Strathern

IVAN R. DEE
CHICAGO

Library of Congress Cataloging-in-Publication Data:
Strathern, Paul, 1940–
    St. Augustine in 90 minutes / Paul Strathern.
      p.   cm. — (Philosophers in 90 minutes)
    Includes bibliographical references and index.
    ISBN 1–56663–149–1 (alk. paper). — ISBN 1–56663–150–5 (pbk. : alk. paper)
    1. Augustine, Saint, Bishop of Hippo. 2. Philosophers—Algeria—Hippo (Extinct city)—Biography. 3. Christian saints—Algeria—Hippo (Extinct city)—Biography. 4. Philosophy, Ancient. 5. Theology, Doctrinal—History—Early church, ca. 30–600. I. Title. II. Series.
B655.Z7S77   1997
189'.2—dc21
                                 96–40321

Contents

ST. AUGUSTINE IN 90 MINUTES

Introduction

The golden age of philosophy came to an end with the death of Aristotle in 322 B.C. What had been a matter of coherent argument now largely degenerated into attitude or commentary. Of the former, there were two main attitudes. Times being what they were, neither of these was optimistic.

The Stoic philosophy was developed by Zeno of Citium, who was born in the early third century B.C. in Cyprus. Zeno was a successful capitalist until he lost all his resources in a shipwreck. He was immediately attracted to the Cynics, who believed that material possessions were of no importance whatsoever. Zeno developed this attitude into his own Stoic philosophy, named after the *stoa* (or pillars) of the arcade in Athens where he taught. Zeno believed in adopting a Stoic attitude to life and claimed that all men are divided into two categories. The first group (Stoics to a man) consist of the wise, who are indifferent to everything except their own wisdom. The rest are fools.

For the Stoics, wisdom meant forswearing the passions and living a life of virtue. This involved self-control, fortitude in the face of adversity, and just behavior.

Stoic philosophy developed over the centuries and eventually became a great hit in Rome, especially among those disillusioned portions of the upper classes who had to endure the whims of recalcitrant emperors. The tragedian Seneca even tried to teach Stoicism to Nero, but the emperor proved temperamentally unsuited to this philosophy.

In the second century A.D. Stoicism was finally adopted by the emperor Marcus Aurelius, who wrote a series of rather pompous and banal meditations on the subject during his long campaign against the trans-Danubian barbarians.

Other similar philosophical attitudes gave rise to the aforementioned Cynics, and to the Skeptics, who believed they knew nothing but saw no contradiction in teaching this.

But the most important attitude other than Stoicism was that adopted by Epicurus, who was born during mid-fourth century B.C., probably in Samos. In later life Epicurus settled in Athens and founded a community that lived in his garden and followed his philosophy. This was known as Epicureanism and was in many ways the opposite of Stoicism. Where Stoics renounced all pleasure, Epicureans believed in living the good life. But Epicurus himself believed that the good life was an extremely simple life— living on bread and water, with perhaps a bit of cheese on holidays. His aim (and initially that of his philosophy) was to achieve a life devoid of all pain. Sex, drunkenness, ambition of any kind, and generally living the high life resulted in headaches, hangovers, and disappointments. These were all a pain, and their causes were thus best avoided. The Romans, who had no feel for such finer points of philosophy, avidly embraced Epicureanism but insisted on their own idea of the good life. This involved a lot more than bread and water. Epicureanism thus became corrupted, acquiring the self-indulgent associations that it retains to this day.

Almost all other philosophers of this period concentrated on the works of their great predecessors. Their activities consisted largely of commenting, analyzing, elaborating, and quibbling. Foremost among these unoriginal critics were followers of Pythagoras and Plato. The greatest of the latter was Plotinus, who developed the religious bent in Platonism and incorporated various mystical features. In the end his philosophy was barely recognizable as Platonism, so it was called Neoplatonism.

The most important intellectual event of the early centuries A.D. was the spread of Christianity. This increasingly stymied any further serious philosophy until the arrival of Augustine.

St. Augustine's Life and Works

"I went to Carthage, where I found myself in the midst of a hissing cauldron of lasciviousness. I ran wild with lust, the abominable things I did: rank depravity, a surfeit of hell's pleasures. Bodily desire like a bubbling swamp and virile sex welling up within me exuded mists. . . ." St. Augustine was a sex maniac. Or so he would have us believe. His famous *Confessions* contain page after page in which he castigates himself for being "the vilest slave of evil passions" and indulging in "the filth of lewdness, hell's black river of lust." But the expectant reader turns the pages with increasing disappointment as he searches for actual examples of "this crazed wantonness." So we don't know exactly what Augustine was up to in the fleshpots of Carthage. My guess is that it wasn't much more than the usual student escapades.

But there's no denying that Augustine had a problem with sex. He had a strong sexual urge and probably enjoyed sex when he was actually doing it. But he was also possessed of an extremely strong mental desire to stay chaste. A few sessions with an understanding analyst would probably have defused the problem—but this would have robbed philosophy of its greatest exponent in almost one and a half millennia. When Augustine arrived on the scene, six hundred years had passed since the death of Aristotle; after Augustine died, it was nearly eight hundred years before the appearance of Thomas Aquinas.

Augustine was born in 354 A.D. in the small town of Thagaste in the Roman province of Numidia (now Souk Ahras in the northeastern hinterland of Algeria). His parents appear to have been a rather boozy middle-class couple. But his hard-drinking father Patricius developed alcoholic symptoms of emotional disintegration in the form of obsessive womanizing and violent outbursts. Whereupon Augustine's mother Monica turned to religion, forswore the demon drink, and transformed her frustrations and disappointments into ambitions for her son.

We know a fair amount about Augustine's youth from the descriptions in his *Confessions*. From the outset Monica appears to have overwhelmed little Augustine, though at no point does Augustine venture a word against his mother, whose obsessive puritan Christianity pervades the book from page one. "Who can recall to me the sins I committed as a baby?" Augustine asks, castigating himself for crying for his mother's milk. "I was indeed a great sinner," he comments, without irony, on his early dislike of lessons at school.

Then, as a teenager, he really goes off the rails. Together with pals from school, he steals the fruit from a pear tree. As a result of this vile iniquity, Augustine indulges in an orgy of self-laceration which continues to the end of the chapter ("foul soul falling from the firmament to expulsion . . . into the depths of the abyss," and so on). He then continues in the same fashion for another *six* chapters before ending: "Can anyone unravel this twisted tangle of knots? I shudder to look at it or think of such abomination." What on earth is this all about? Readers of a psychological bent may find symbolic overtones in the young lad "shaking down the fruit from the tree," but this would be a shallow and uninformative explanation. The real villain of the piece here was definitely Mom.

There is no doubt that Monica ruled the family's home life. She even managed to persuade the hapless Patricius to convert to Christianity, almost certainly in a fit of alcoholic remorse, the year before he died. And when it became apparent that young Augustine had inherited some of his father's unspeakable habits, he was banished from the family home. But only briefly: Monica did not wish to let him out of her clutches.

Meanwhile Augustine continued to wrestle with his Problem. In despair he would even occasionally turn to God, imploring him in touching

14

fashion, "Lord, give me chastity—but not yet." He didn't want God to "cure me too soon of the disease of lust, which I wanted satisfied, not quelled."

Augustine was an extremely bright boy, and Monica had great ambitions for him. Before Patricius died he had scraped together enough money for the boy to continue his education at Carthage. Here, away from Mother, Augustine had a number of experiences in the bordellos and developed a taste for the theatre (later described in the *Confessions* as "a loathsome mange, which swells and festers with hideous pus. What miserable delirium!"). He then settled down to live with a woman, with whom he was to share a long and faithful loving relationship. She even had "an accidental son" by Augustine. (Nothing is said against her personally in the *Confessions*; it's what they repeatedly and enjoyably did together that upset him.)

But Augustine wasn't just a prig with a problem. The turbulence that drove him to such (alleged) extremes of lewdness and such extremes of (purely literary) self-abasement also drove him with equal force to discover the truth about himself. Why did he behave in such a way? How could he be so utterly and despicably vile and polluted and at the same time yearn with equal longing for purity?

The psychology that might have reduced him to shallow normality was not available, and the Christianity offered by his mother appeared too simple to satisfy his demanding intellect. What he needed was a convincing explanation of his plight, sufficiently profound for him to believe. He began reading Cicero and was at once attracted to philosophy. It was Cicero, a graduate of Plato's Academy, who taught him the difficult business of how to think properly. But Cicero offered no solution.

Augustine found what he was looking for in Manichaeism. This quasi-Christian sect had been founded a century earlier by a Persian named Mani, who had claimed to be the Holy Ghost and had ended by being crucified by fire worshipers. Manichaeism was essentially dualistic, its adherents believing that the world was a product of the conflict between Good and Evil (or Light and Darkness). Man's soul consisted of light, entrapped by darkness from which it must seek to free itself. This was a belief tailor-made for Augustine in his present state, even if it had been proscribed as a heresy by the Christian church. Augustine embraced Manichaeism with open arms.

Mother was not pleased when Augustine arrived home after his four years of study in Carthage. The mistress and child she could accept (they could be dealt with later), but Manichaeism was another matter. This grieved her heart, and she saw no point in disguising the fact. Meanwhile Augustine began teaching rhetoric in his home town, and became interested in astronomy. But Augustine, now twenty, remained ambitious, and a year later he returned to Carthage, where he worked in the university as a visiting teacher. Unfortunately the times were changing and the students were out of control. Discipline problems became so great that teaching was virtually impossible. Augustine decided to set off with his mistress and young son to look for work in Rome.

By now Augustine was beginning to have intellectual doubts about Manichaeism. The latest findings of astronomy did not accord with the mythological explanations of the heavens offered by the Manichaeans. Augustine was visited by Bishop Faustus, the Manichaean scholar, and together they discussed these matters. But in the end the good-natured bishop was forced to confess that he had no answer to these problems, which set Augustine pondering.

Mother didn't approve of the projected trip to Rome, and she came to Carthage to say so. Before the boat sailed there was a scene on the quayside, with Monica "clinging to me with all her strength in the hope that I would either come home or take her with me." Augustine finally persuaded Monica that the boat would not sail until next morning, and she went off to visit a nearby shrine to St. Cyprian. Augustine then secretly set sail under cover of darkness, "leaving her alone to her prayers and her tears."

In Rome Augustine continued to mix with Manichaeans. Despite his doubts, he remained convinced by their doctrine that it was not us who sinned but some other darker nature that entrapped the soul. He continued teaching, and within a year his intellectual brilliance had been noticed. He was offered a post as professor of rhetoric at Milan.

Milan had recently replaced Rome as the administrative capital of the Roman Empire, which was in the process of splitting into its eastern and western halves. The empire was entering one of the more exotic periods of its long decline, with the crowning of teenage emperors and the like. (The army had recently excelled itself by proclaiming a four-year-old as emperor, but this example of military intelligence had been politely overlooked; a degenerate adult had briefly been put forward in his stead.) The present emperor now resided in Milan, but the most influential figure in the city was Bishop—later to become Saint—Ambrose. His power was so great that he had recently ordered the Emperor Theodosius to perform a penance after he had been responsible for a massacre in Thessalonica.

Ambrose was one of the ablest minds in Christendom, and his sermons attracted large audiences. Augustine went to hear one and was at once disabused of two prejudices he had held toward Christianity. He saw that this religion *could* be embraced by a man of great intellect. He also saw that the Bible was a more profound book than he had previously realized, and that it was not always to be understood literally.

A year after Augustine's arrival in Milan, his mother finally caught up with him. By now Augustine was able to reassure Monica that he was no longer a Manichaean; but he was not yet a Christian either. He still had large ambitions "for fame and wealth and marriage." Monica seems to have been all in favor, and soon persuaded him it was time he found himself a proper wife. A girl of suitable family was selected and they became engaged, despite the fact that she was so young he would have to wait for two years before they could legally marry. But there was a price to pay for all this. "The woman with whom I had been living [for over twelve years] was torn from my side as an obstacle to my marriage and this was a blow which crushed my heart to bleeding, because I loved her dearly." Augustine's mistress—who remains nameless throughout the *Confessions*—was forced to leave her son with Augustine and was sent back to Africa "vowing never to give herself to another man." (This last remark is usually taken as a token of her undying love for Augustine, though women may interpret it differently.) Augustine soon found the prospect of a two-year wait before his marriage quite unendurable, and he took another mistress—yet despite this he remained "devastated" by the loss of his first mistress.

More than ever, Augustine now found himself tormented by "the problem of evil." He could no longer believe in the Manichaeans, largely because of their intellectual inferiority. They appeared unable to answer his questions on astronomy or explain the problem of his irrepressible sexual impulse. Yet there seemed to be no alternative to their dualistic interpretation of the world. The soul of Light within him remained helplessly in the grip of Darkness beyond his control. Yet the very notion of dualism seemed more and more unacceptable to him. Then he discovered the writings of Plotinus.

Plotinus had been born in Alexandria at the beginning of the third century A.D. Like many brilliant critics, he thought he understood what he had read better than the author himself. In this case Plotinus was convinced that he understood the philosophy of Plato much better than Plato himself had managed. In his attempt to explain what Plato had really meant to say, Plotinus transformed Plato's original theories into what came to be called Neoplatonism. Into the container of Platonic theory Plotinus poured a cocktail of features from Pythagoras, Aristotle, and the Stoics, adding a mystical twist of his own.

Like Plato, the Neoplatonists saw ultimate reality and goodness as transcendent. The highest reality was the One. Things emanated from this unity in a descending order of reality, worth, and integration. Evil arose from the unfocused matter at the bottom of the scale, farthest from the One. This meant there was no need for any dualism to describe the nature of evil, as required by the Manichaeans. For the Neoplatonists, evil was merely the absence of good. It was the farthest thing from the greatest reality of the One, and thus the least real thing of all. Here was the answer to Augustine's unacceptable dualism, an answer that solved once and for all the problem of evil. (It barely existed.)

In many ways Neoplatonism at this stage of its development resembled a philosophic version of Christianity, but without a Christian God. All this time Augustine was moving closer and closer to the Christianity of his mother; in an attempt to see his way through to the truth, he even began reading the Epistles of St. Paul. Still he could not bring himself to take the ultimate step.

By August 388 A.D. this spiritual crisis had brought Augustine to the verge of a nervous breakdown. One day, in a turmoil of anger and anguish at his state of indecision, he sought relief in the quiet of his garden. For a while he tore at his hair and banged his fists against his forehead. Eventually he flung himself down beneath a fig tree and gave way to his tears. Then slowly he became aware of the singsong voice of a child in a neighboring house chanting, "Tolle, lege. Tolle, lege." (Take it and read it.) At first he thought the child's chanting was part of a game, then suddenly he realized "this could only be a divine command to open my book of the Scriptures and read the first lines my eyes should light upon." Immediately he ceased sobbing, got up, and hurried over to the copy of St. Paul's Epistles that he had left on a nearby bench. He seized the book, opened it, and read the first words he saw: "... not in rioting and drunkenness, not in lust and lewdness, not in strife and envy. Instead, take unto you the Lord Jesus Christ, and spend no more time thinking of the flesh in order to fulfil its lusts." Augustine was converted. He returned to the house and told his mother what had happened, and she was overjoyed.

Many Christians through the centuries have regarded Augustine's conversion to Christianity as a miracle, but it's worth pointing out that if you look in St. Paul's Epistles the voice of God has little option but to speak to you in Christian terms. Had Augustine looked into the Upanishads or the Egyptian Book of the Dead, he might have come across a very similar passage which exhorted him to become a Hindu or worship the Sun God Re.

Augustine now resigned his teaching post and gave up the idea of marriage. On the Saturday before Easter 387, he and his son Adeodatus were baptized by Ambrose in Milan. Augustine and his mother then decided to return to Numidia. As they were about to embark at the port of Ostia, Monica caught a fever. Augustine did his best to nurse her, but her mission was now complete, and she died.

Years later Augustine's mother was canonized, and she is now the patron saint of married women. Her sacred remains were transferred to Rome, where they reside appropriately in the church of Sant'Agostino. Today she is most widely remembered through the name of a laidback beachside suburb of Los Angeles, whose inhabitants' behavior would certainly not have met with her approval. The demise of Santa Monica brings to an end the narrative part of

Augustine's *Confessions*, which he was to write a decade later.

Augustine sailed back to Africa and returned home to Thagaste, accompanied by a number of devout friends. Here they set up a community for living a monastic life, and Augustine spent most of his time writing and studying. Despite all his protestations of passion and sin, Augustine was essentially a contemplative type. This was the kind of life he enjoyed best, and it was almost certainly during this period that he did the thinking that laid the foundations of his philosophy.

Augustine had been particularly struck by the mystical elements of Neoplatonism and the idea that man's innermost spirit links him to supreme reality. Plotinus believed that to reach the supreme One, the ultimate reality, we must look deeply inside ourselves. This had been Augustine's experience, and he now sought to reconcile the doctrine of Plotinus with the Christianity of St. Paul. Eventually this led him to reconcile Neoplatonism as a whole with the teachings of the Bible.

The fusion of these two doctrines, which were far from complementary, was to be Augustine's major contribution to philosophy. This not only provided Christianity with a strong intellectual backing but tied it to the Greek tradition of philosophy. In this way Christianity managed to keep the flame of philosophy burning, however dimly, through the Dark Ages.

In the course of this work Augustine produced many philosophic ideas of his own. The Greek thought of Plotinus, much like our thinking today, could not accept that something can be created out of nothing, as in the Bible. For the Neoplatonists the One was timeless and without purpose. In order to make Neoplatonism consistent with the Book of Genesis, Augustine introduced into it the creation and "the will of God that good things should be." But here he was faced with a difficulty. How could the timeless One (which had now become God) operate in time?

This problem led Augustine to propose a theory of time far in advance of any ancient Greek thinking on this matter, and not seriously challenged until Kant's theory thirteen centuries later (which some see as a mere development of Augustine's original idea). According to Augustine, God exists outside time, which started only with the creation of the world. There is thus no validity to the question, What happened before the world was created? For Augustine, time is subjective, existing in the human mind as an aspect of our way of seeing. We cannot see the world in any other way—though ultimate reality is not subject to time.

This essentially blind, unknowing subjectivism led Augustine to question the very basis of subjective knowledge. What can we possibly know of ultimate reality if it is beyond us in every sense? Indeed, what do we know at all? Nothing in certainty—except that we exist and that we are thinking. These ideas in Augustine's *Soliloquies* anticipate by more than eleven centuries Descartes's celebrated "Cogito ergo Sum" (I think therefore I am), which was to revolutionize philosophy. Fortunately this passage was overlooked, or not acted upon, by Augustine's medieval successors—or they would probably have ended up burned at the stake.

In 391 Augustine visited Hippo (formerly Bône, now Annaba, on the northeast coast of Algeria). Here Bishop Valerius persuaded him that he should become ordained. In order to do this, Augustine was forced to leave his community. Within five years the aging Valerius appointed Augustine as his assistant bishop of Hippo, and when Valerius died a year later Augustine was called upon to take over all his pastoral work.

In those days the bishop was not only the senior local priest but also the city's theology professor and civil judge. Despite these onerous duties, Augustine continued to write prolifically. During the two years after his appointment as bishop he wrote innumerable pamphlets and sermons and kept up a wide correspondence. He also produced his *Confessions*. As well as outlining the sexual agonies of his youth, the *Confessions* contain one of the most profound statements of faith in all Christian writing. They also contain an outline of Augustine's philosophy, including his original theory of time.

Unfortunately not all of Augustine's vast literary output was of such high quality. Like many converts, Augustine became obsessed with the niceties of church doctrine. Much of his precious time was wasted conducting vituperative campaigns against deviations from orthodox thinking. The Manichaean heresy, which he knew so well, became a particular object of fulmination ("this unspeakable mental excretia"). But this wasn't the only heresy around.

The Donatists, for example, were a Christian sect which came into prominence in North Africa in the early fourth century, when they broke with the Roman church. The Donatists held that the church must remain absolutely free of state interference. This would have been all very well, but a central part of their program was to bring about a revolution against the state—which would be followed by the arrival of the Four Horsemen of the Apocalypse and the end of the world. This social program was aided by peasant warriors called Circumcellions.

The Donatists welcomed hostility, as this demonstrated the evil of the world. They believed in a life of penance and persecution, which if they were lucky would end in martyrdom. This made the Donatists extremely difficult to stamp out, as every action taken against them was welcomed and only confirmed their views. By the time Augustine became Bishop of Hippo a large portion of the Christians in North Africa had gone over to this heresy, and Augustine spent much of his time writing polemics condemning them in the fiercest terms.

Later in his life Augustine also became a scourge of the Pelagians. This heretical sect had been started by a Welsh monk named Morgan (this name comes from the Gaelic for sailor, which translated into Latin as Pelagius). When Brother Morgan arrived in Rome, his upright Welsh spirit was appalled by the moral laxity of the priesthood, which tended to take a rather more easy-going, Mediterranean view of its vows. But Morgan soon detected the cause of the trouble. One day he heard a sermon in which a bishop referred to a passage in Augustine's *Con-*

fessions (whose dwelling on unspecific salaciousness had soon stimulated sales and imaginations throughout Christendom). The passage quoted by the bishop explained Augustine's view that goodness is not possible without the intervention of divine grace, a doctrine verging on predestination. Morgan realized that many were using this doctrine as an excuse for moral lassitude. There was no point in making an effort to be good if this depended upon the intervention of divine grace.

Morgan opposed this view with a doctrine of his own. This stated that there was no such thing as original sin, and that people were capable of earning a place in heaven without intervention from God's grace. Such pernicious heresy raised a storm of protest, not least from Augustine, who at once set about defending his ethical theory. He began writing a series of heated polemics, savaging the evil Welshman and his growing band of followers.

Augustine wasted a great deal of his time pouring out such propaganda. He soon became renowned throughout Christendom as a stickler for orthodoxy. (According to Augustine, even unbaptized infants were condemned to everlasting damnation.) One cannot help but wonder what caused a great thinker like Augustine to spend so much of his time and energy on such arrant nonsense. Yet this was not just some individual psychological quirk; it was symptomatic of a collective mania that was to grip the church for many centuries to come. From the perspective of history we can only marvel at the perversity of Augustine and the other great European minds of the period who spent their time in similar fashion. The Roman Empire was in the last vestiges of collapse before the Dark Ages, yet the finest intellects in Christendom were busily engaged in bitter controversies over the intervention of divine grace, whether unbaptized infants went to hell, and the need for chastity.

In 410 A.D. Alaric and the victorious Visigoths enthusiastically set about the Sack of Rome. These were the first foreign invaders to have penetrated the city walls for nearly eight hundred years. The fall of Rome was quickly blamed on the loss of faith in the ancient gods, whose worship had recently been banned by the Emperor Theodosius in favor of Christianity. As long as Jupiter had been worshiped, Rome had ruled, and now look what had happened. It was all the Christians' fault.

This argument struck a nerve with Augustine, and he was determined to counter it. His reply was the *City of God*, a great work of theology and philosophy which is unfortunately even more unreadable today than his *Confessions*. In the *City of God* Augustine sets forth the first Christian view of history, allowing Christians to accept the fall of Rome as part of the divine order of things. Against the Earthly City, whose inhabitants delight in the temporal world, he posits the City of God, a community inspired by the love of God through the intercession of divine grace. The City of God had a purely spiritual existence and was not to be identified with anywhere on earth, even the holy city of Rome. These ideas were to have a profound effect on the medieval church and later even played their part in the Reformation.

In the course of the *City of God* Augustine

produces a number of ingenious arguments. Christians should not sorrow at the sight of the victorious Goths going unpunished for the Sack of Rome. (The Visigoths, a subgroup of the Goths, had in fact done the deed, but Augustine chose to ignore such niceties when referring to these bloodthirsty barbarians.) Augustine assured his readers that the gross misdeeds of the Goths would be punished when they went to meet their maker. After all, if every sin were punished on earth, what would be the point of having a Last Judgment?

Owing to Augustine's usual preoccupations, the *City of God* also contains several prolonged passages about sex. These will strike the modern reader as implausible, hilarious, or the last word on lustful practices, depending upon his or her point of view. Augustine even explains how Adam and Eve could easily have had sex before the Fall (though he stresses that they certainly did not). This could have taken place as an act of will, without accompanying lust. As Augustine recognized, this would have left Adam's organ unstimulated by desire, so he provides an argument demonstrating how the necessary mechanical feat could have been achieved by willpower alone. Anyone who believes that philosophy is no laughing matter should read this passage. (See the extract in the Writings section.)

Augustine also discusses whether virgins raped by the Goths at the Sack of Rome remained virtuous, a question that caused much vexation at the time. In Augustine's view they did, since chastity was a virtue of the mind. But they did not remain virtuous if they had enjoyed the experience. Augustine adds that God may have permitted these rapes because the women concerned were too proud of their chastity. Where much of Augustine's theology may now appear meaningless or boring, such passages remain as offensive today as they must have been to any right-thinking person then. This is not to doubt Augustine's integrity. If he too had been raped by the Goths, this probably would not have changed his thinking on the matter.

It took Augustine thirteen years to write the *City of God*, which he completed in 426 A.D., at the age of seventy-two. Throughout this period he had continued with his duties as Bishop of Hippo, also producing hundreds of sermons and persisting with his vigorous persecution of heretics. (After the fall of Rome, Pelagius-Morgan arrived in North Africa and began preaching his heresies on Augustine's home ground, thus providing a constant stimulus and source of inspiration.) Yet despite Augustine's public office and high esteem throughout Christendom, he remained essentially an isolated scholar going about his self-appointed tasks. During his last years he is said to have been the only man in Hippo who possessed a book. Such was the city from which the first great Christian philosopher, St. Augustine of Hippo, was to take his name.

The site of Hippo is now occupied by the Algerian industrial port of Annaba. As the ferry makes its way in from Marseilles one sees the mosques and tawdry colonial boulevards beneath the haze from the large steel plant. At the edge of the expanding city, high-rise flats extend up the hillside. But beyond the outskirts the landscape remains much as it must have been almost sixteen centuries ago in Augustine's day—

the inland hills above the city dotted with groves of cork trees, and the shoreline of the bay sweeping round toward the cape under the high blue African sky.

The nondescript ruins of ancient Hippo are twenty minutes' walk south from the city center, near the sprawling steel plant. High on the hillside above the ruins stands a tasteless French-built basilica, dating from the turn of the century. This is dedicated to St. Augustine. Nothing else of the great Christian saint remains here. Yet this modern Muslim city is now experiencing a reawakening of religious fanaticism which Augustine would certainly have recognized: its fundamentalist aspects mirror many of his own preoccupations. (Had Augustine lived to see the rise of Mohammedanism, however, it would doubtless have received the same lengthy shrift as the Manichaeans, Donatists, and Pelagians.)

During the last years of Augustine's life the collapse of the Roman Empire continued apace. In 428 A.D. the Vandals invaded the North African provinces, and by May 430 they had reached the gates of Hippo. Four months after the beginning of the year-long siege, Augustine died, on August 28, 430. His saint's day is now celebrated on the anniversary of this date. Augustine was widely regarded as a saint immediately after his death. (Canonization as a formal process occurred only at the end of the first millennium.)

The Vandals soon overran the whole of North Africa, and in 497 their king, Thrasamund, expelled the Catholic bishops from Numidia. When the bishops left they took the body of Augustine with them to Sardinia. Here it remained until the Saracen invasions of the eighth century, when King Luitprand of the Lombards ransomed Augustine's relics and had them brought by his knights to Pavia in Italy, where they remain to this day. As you walk down the Strada Nuovo, you come to the beautifully named San Pietro in Ciel d'Oro (St. Peter in the Golden Heavens). Inside this twelfth-century Lombard-Romanesque church, by the high altar, you can see the ornate marble reliquary that contains the mortal remains of St. Augustine of Hippo.

After St. Augustine

By the time of Augustine's death the Western Empire of the old Roman Empire was in its last throes. The Vandals finally overran the African provinces in 439; Rome was again sacked, this time by the Vandals, in 455. A year later the child emperor Romulus Augustulus was deposed, and the Roman half of the Roman Empire became extinct. The Dark Ages was beginning.

Ancient learning in western Europe was to be preserved through this period by the Christian monastic tradition. This managed to survive, largely in isolation to begin with, but eventually infiltrating its message through missionaries into the embryo feudal kingdoms of Europe.

Meanwhile the Eastern Empire continued in the Balkans and Asia Minor, with its capital at Constantinople. The Byzantine Empire (as it came to be known) developed the more mystical and avaricious elements of the old Roman Empire, but few of its virtues. In 529 A.D. the emperor Justinian finally suppressed all "pagan" Hellenistic culture and closed Plato's Academy in Athens. Many historians regard this event as the definitive start of the Dark Ages.

Inevitably this was not a good time for philosophers, who require a stable civilized society with a tradition of learning and leisure. (Philosophy seldom flourishes without an idle educated class.) The first thinker of any note to appear in western Europe after Augustine was Boethius, who died about a century after Augustine, at Pavia in Italy. Boethius is best remembered for his "golden volume," *Consolation of Philosophy*. During the medieval era this was to become the most widely read book apart from the Bible, and Boethius was mistakenly regarded by many as an even greater Christian philosopher than Augustine.

Consolation of Philosophy was written while Boethius was confined to a cell under sentence of death. (This more extreme form of leisure has also provided a stimulus to philosophic thought through the ages. Most original philosophers merely faced the *prospect* of such stimulating seclusion, achieving it only if their originality was recognized during their lifetime.)

According to Boethius, the only true philosophers were Socrates, Plato, and Aristotle, though his own austere moral doctrine more closely resembles that of the Stoics. In *Consolation of Philosophy* Boethius conducts a dialogue with Philosophy—which answers his prose questions in rhyming verse:

"If thou wouldst see
God's laws with purest mind
Thy sight on heaven fixed must be."

Boethius's philosophy is Platonism pure and unadulterated, with none of the mystical Neoplatonism of Plotinus. The tenets of Christianity do not actually appear, but Boethius's Platonist argument in no way contradicts them. This shows how similar much of Christianity was to Platonist thinking, though if Boethius had extended his comparison he would have come up against several glaring contradictions—such as the conflicting views of creation held by Platonists (*ex nihilo nihil fit*: nothing out of nothing comes) and Christians (God created the world). Augustine had recognized many of these problems and dealt with them a century earlier, thus paving the way for essentially Platonist thinkers such as Boethius to consider themselves orthodox Christians. This was no mean feat in an era during which Christianity continued to be riven by schisms and heresies. Ironically, in the end it was heresy that was to cause Boethius's downfall. He was sentenced to death by his erstwhile friend Theodoric the Great, the Arian Christian king of the Ostrogoths, for refusing to accept the Arian heresy. According to Arianism, Christ was not divine and thus had no direct knowledge of God.

Boethius's *Consolation of Philosophy* popularized Platonist thought among the medieval monastic classes (or at least its literate minority). This elite was thus kept in touch with genuine philosophical thinking, even if it was forbidden from indulging in such dangerous practices. If Augustine hadn't conjured Platonism out of the Christian hat, it is doubtful whether Christian thinking would have included any philosophy worthy of the name. Except for Augustine it is almost certain that Platonic thought—and thus the entire tradition of Western philosophy— would have been condemned as pagan (which it undeniably was) or at least as heretical (ditto).

The first real philosopher of the medieval era was John Scotus Erigena. He was born at the start of the ninth century and probably worked for a time at the court of the French king Charles the Bald. John Scotus conceived of man as a microcosm of the universe. With his senses he perceived the world, with his reason he worked out the causes and effects of things, and with his intellect he contemplated God. More important, John Scotus believed in the efficacy of purely philosophical argument. Reason (i.e., philosophy) was just as good a way of arriving at the truth as theology (i.e., revelation or faith). And as they were both ways of arriving at the truth, they never really contradicted each other. But when they appeared to be in conflict, it was best to rely upon reason. Scotus maintained that true religion was true philosophy—but true philosophy was also true religion. This caused a furor in the church, and was condemned at no less than two councils as "Scots porridge."

Despite this attitude, philosophy managed to survive into the Middle Ages. The continuing popularity of Boethius's *Consolation of Philosophy* and Augustine's *Confessions* ensured that throughout the Middle Ages the monastic tradition remained in touch with the Platonist tradition. The main body of the *Confessions* may have been devoted to Augustine's spiritual vicissitudes on the way to sainthood, but its last three books (XI–XIII) deal largely with philosophical problems. "How did the world begin?" "What is time?" "Do the past and the future exist?" are just some of the problems he raises and attempts to answer. And those who were tempted to read further into his works could discover many rich seams of genuine philosophical argument among the diatribes against heretics, explanations of the mechanics of sex without lust, and so forth.

Augustine was to have a profound influence upon several leading thinkers of the medieval era. The most important of these was probably St. Anselm, the eleventh-century founder of Scholasticism, the pseudophilosophy that was to reign supreme throughout the Middle Ages. Scholasticism was basically an attempt to build a body of genuine philosophical thought upon a foundation of rigid religious dogma. The former was subject to philosophical argument, the latter was not. Philosophical argument was wide-ranging and conducted with nit-picking accuracy, but if one inadvertently strayed into questioning dogma he was liable to end up burned at the stake. The chief object of philosophical debate soon became to demonstrate that your opponent had made the cardinal error of contradicting dogma. Philosophy became a dangerous power game for the brilliant and ambitious few. (Psychologists continue to regard this urge to dominate as the *real* basis of philosophical argument, with the object being the traumatic humiliation of the defeated ego. And this is not so far-fetched if one regards philosophical argument as analogous to chess. If, on the other hand, one regards it as anything remotely related to the truth . . .)

Such considerations are not as frivolous and irrelevant as they might appear. And once again Augustine has a hand in this. The ancient Greeks simply agreed to differ on philosophical matters. Diogenes the Stoic ridiculed the members of Plato's Academy, but that was as far as it went. With the merging of philosophy and Christianity, things changed. Augustine was not engaged in purely academic debate when he attacked the Donatist and Pelagian heresies. They were splitting Christendom, and he wished to destroy them. The most convincing way of doing this was to destroy their philosophical basis by reasonable argument. Such methods are as recognizable now as they were in Augustine's time: his power game with Morgan (Pelagius) was little different from the *philosophical* dispute between Stalin and Trotsky over their differing interpretations of the Communist gospel. The loser was judged a heretic, with him and his followers being rooted out. Most propaganda battles between rival dogmas have been concerned to win over hearts and *minds*.

When philosophy (and its methods) are used in this way, the psychologists are right: philosophy becomes a power game. But this gives rise to a fundamental question. And Augustine, who helped usher in this method, seems not to have been aware of it. When is philosophy not used (or misused) in this way? Are there any circumstances in which philosophy is not a power game, albeit one that it is conducted according to the most rigid rules, which are intended to direct us toward the truth? Anyone who feels confident enough to answer this question should ponder the words of Xenophanes: "No one knows, or will ever know, the truth about the gods and everything; for if one chanced to say the whole truth, nevertheless one would never know it." This accords with much twentieth-century philosophy, as it did with certain elements of Greek philosophy, and has done with

skeptical philosophy through the centuries between. Yet if we cannot know the truth, the psychological argument becomes all but irresistible
—he who musters the best argument wins. Fortunately we now recognize that philosophy is as
much about the rules of this argument as it is
about who wins.

Augustine would not have seen it this way.
Largely as a result of such an attitude, philosophy was misused throughout the Middle Ages. It
was coopted as Christian propaganda and was
acceptable only as such. An atheist or a Muslim
simply could not have taken part in a philosophical argument in western Europe. It thus comes
as little surprise that some of the best philosophy of this period was produced by Muslims
(Averroës and Avicenna), and that Scholasticism
was finally brought to an end by Descartes, who
used the arguments of an atheist (though pru-
dently denying that he was one).

Another major figure influenced by Augustine was the thirteenth-century Franciscan St.
Bonaventura. Consciously following in the foot-
steps of Augustine, Bonaventura sought to incor-

50

porate into Scholasticism various elements of Plato that were in fact incompatible with Christianity—going so far as to include some that even Augustine had considered beyond the pale. But he drew the line at incorporating Aristotelianism, which he considered to be directly opposed to Scholasticism. In so far as Aristotelianism helped introduce an element of scientific thought into Scholasticism, Bonaventura was to be proved utterly right.

St. Bonaventura's best-known contemporary was Duns Scotus (1266–1308)—not to be confused with John Scotus Erigena, who had died four centuries earlier. He was less influenced by Augustine, despite using copious quotes from Augustine's works to support his arguments. But he was more important than St. Bonaventura as a philosopher, even though his name was the origin of our word *dunce* (a calumny coined by his enemies). At one stage Duns Scotus was forced to flee Paris for his life—after proposing, contrary to official papal doctrine, that Mary's Immaculate Conception did not involve her in original sin. This episode illustrates not only the dangers facing thinkers in the Middle Ages but the metaphysical depths to which current debate had sunk. Many consider Duns Scotus to have been the finest speculative mind of the Middle Ages; it is a tragedy to see such a talent reduced to squabbles over metaphysical mumbo jumbo. Yet he also made many important contributions. These are mainly elaborations of (and solutions to) difficulties arising from the Platonism first introduced by Augustine. For instance, Duns Scotus's distinction between the essential and accidental properties of a thing marked a major logical advance. A book's pages are essential to its identity, but the color of its binding is simply accidental. Arguments of this caliber had been almost nonexistent since Aristotle, fifteen hundred years earlier. Duns Scotus demonstrated that logic could be used as a practical tool— though no use was made of this for several centuries, owing to the unscientific tenor of the age.

Duns Scotus's definitions of the things we can know without proof point ahead to the period when philosophy at last shed the stifling weight of theology. According to Duns Scotus there are three distinct kinds of knowledge without proof: first, principles which we know by themselves; second, things we know by experience; and third, the actions we take ourselves.

Duns Scotus became an enemy of Thomas Aquinas (c1225–1274), the greatest of all the medieval philosophers. Aquinas was not influenced to any great extent by Augustine, but his major contribution was remarkably similar. Where Augustine squared Platonist thought with Christian dogma, Aquinas managed to reconcile the works of Aristotle with the current teachings of the church. Many of these works had only recently resurfaced in western Europe, largely as a result of Muslim philosophers such as Averroës. This completed the circle for philosophy. The finest of ancient Greek thought had now been incorporated into Scholasticism. The result was disastrous. The essentially clear, fluid nature of Greek speculative thinking was frozen in the rigid glacier of Christian metaphysics, whose forward pace was all but undetectable. The result was a formidable wonder, comparable in proportion and splendor to a Gothic cathedral.

You were meant to view this sight as a tourist, absorbing it in awe. Those who wished to know more could always join a conducted tour. But anyone who attempted to explore this wonder on his own might disappear down some crevice of heresy, never to be seen again. Augustine cannot be blamed for such an outcome, but it was he who first set philosophy in this direction.

From St. Augustine's Writings

Give me chastity—but not yet!
—*Confessions*, Book VIII, Chap. 7

For many, total abstinence is easier than perfect moderation.
—*On the Good of Marriage*, Chap. 21

Therefore it is true to say that when you had not created anything, time did not exist, because you created time. And there is no time which exists eternally with you, because you never change; for if time never changed, it would not be time.

What, then, is time? There is no quick and easy answer to this, for it is no simple matter to understand what time is, let alone find words to explain it. Yet in our conversation, no word is more familiar to us, or more easily recognized, than the word "time." We definitely understand what this word means, both when we use it ourselves and when we hear it used by others.

What, then, is time? I know perfectly well what it is—so long as no one asks me; but as soon as I am asked what it is and try to explain it, I am nonplussed. However, I can say with confidence that if nothing passed, there would be no past time; if nothing were going to happen, there would be no future time; and if nothing *were*, there would be no present time.

So with these three divisions of time, how can two of them—the past and the future—*be*, when the past no longer is, and the future is not yet? As for the present, if it were always present and never moved on to become the past, it would not be time but eternity. Therefore, if the present is time only because of the fact that it moves on to become the past, how can we say

56

that even the present *is*, when the reason why it *is* is that it is *not to be*? In other words, we cannot properly say that time *exists*, except because of its impending state of *nonexistence.*

—*Confessions*, Book XI, Chap. 14

Love the sinner, but hate the sin.

—Letter 211 in *Patrologiae Latinae* (1845), Vol. 33

So I muddied the stream of friendship with the filth of lewdness and clouded its clear waters with hell's black river of lust. And yet, despite such putrid depravity, I was vain enough to harbor an ambition to succeed in the world. I also fell in love, which was a trap of my own making. My God, God of mercy, how good you were to me, for you mixed much bitterness in that cup of pleasure. My love was returned, and I became chained in the shackles of its consummation. Even in the midst of my joys I was embroiled in tribulation, lashed by the cruel rods of jealousy, suspicion, fear, anger, and bitter argument.

—*Confessions*, Book III, Chap. 1

I was attracted to the theatre, because the plays reflected my own sad plight and were sparks which set my feelings ablaze. Why do men enjoy feeling sad at the sight of tragedy and sufferings on stage, although they would be pitifully unhappy if they had to endure such things themselves? Yet they watch plays because they hope to be made sad, and the feeling of sadness is what they enjoy. What pitiful madness this is! The more a man suffers such sorrows himself, the more he is moved by the sight of them on stage. Yet when he suffers himself, we call it misery; when he suffers out of sympathy for others, we call it pity.

—*Confessions*, Book III, Chap. 2

There was no extreme of heat or cold in paradise, and its inhabitants experienced no desire or fear which might obstruct their goodwill. . . . A man and his wife maintained a faithful partnership based on love and mutual respect, and faultless observance of the commandment. . . . When humanity was blessed with such ease and plenty, it would have been possible for the seed of children to be sown unaccompanied by foul lust. The sexual organs would have been stimulated into necessary activity by willpower alone, just as the will controls other organs. Then, without being goaded on by the allurement of passion, the husband could have relaxed upon his wife's bosom in complete peace of mind and bodily tranquillity . . . that part of his body not activated by tumultuous passion, but brought into service by the deliberate use of power when the need arose, the seed dispatched into the womb with no loss of his wife's virginity. . . . So the two sexes could have come together for impregnation and conception by an act of will, rather than by lustful cravings.

—*City of God*, Book XIV, Chap. 26

sex without sin!

59

AUGUSTINE: You who wish to know, do you know that you exist?

REASON: I do.

A: How do you know this?

R: I do not know.

A: Do you feel yourself to be simple or complex?

R: I do not know.

A: Do you feel that you are self-moved?

R: I do not know.

A: Do you know that you think?

R: I do.

—*Soliloquies*, Book II, Chap. I

The certainty that I exist, that I know this, and that I am glad of it, is known independently of any imaginary fantasy or contradiction.

With regard to these truths, I am not afraid of any arguments put forward by the Academics. If they say, "What if you are mistaken?" I reply, "Even if I am mistaken, I still exist." A nonexistent being cannot be mistaken. Therefore I must exist if I am mistaken. Since my being mistaken proves that I exist, how can I be mistaken when I think that I exist, if my mistake confirms my existence? Therefore I must exist in order to be mistaken, then, even if I am mistaken, there is no denying that I am not mistaken in my knowledge that I exist. Therefore I am also not mistaken in knowing that I know. For in the same way that I know I exist, I also know that I know. And when I am glad about these two facts, I can add with equal certainty the fact of that gladness to the things that I know. For I am not mistaken about the fact of my gladness, because I am not mistaken about the things which I love. Even if these things are illusory, it would still be a fact that I love the illusions.

—*City of God*, Book XI, Chap. 26

You certainly will not deny there is an immutable truth, containing all things that are immutably true, which you cannot claim is yours or mine or any other man's. In some wonderful way, an ineffable and universal light is, so to speak, present and made manifest equally to all.

But who can say that what is present to all who reason and understand belongs in any real sense to the nature of any individual? For remember what we said just now about the bodily senses. Namely, that what we all perceive with our eyes or our ears, such as colors and sounds, do not belong to our individual eyes or ears, but are there for all. In the same way, you cannot say that those things which we all apprehend, with our own individual minds, are anything to do with these individual minds. For what the eyes of two people see at the same time cannot be said to pertain to the eyes of either one of them, but in fact consist of some third thing to which the gaze of both is turned.

—*De Libero Arbitrio Voluntatis,*
Book 1, Chap. 12

God would never have created any man, let alone an angel, in the foreknowledge of his future evil state, without simultaneously bearing in mind the overall good of the world. He understood how he would make use of such creatures to heighten the course of world history, in much the same way as antithesis heightens the beauty of a poem.

—*City of God*, Book XI, Chap. 18

Love and do what you will.

—*In Epistolium Joannis ad Parthos*, tractatus 7, sec. 8

In reply to those who ask, "What was God doing before he created heaven and earth?" I do not say, "He was preparing hell for people who ask awkward questions." This only evades the point. . . .

A fickle-minded man . . . might ask why you . . . should have been idle and permitted countless ages to pass before you eventually set about the great task of creation. My advice to such a person is to wake up and think properly, for his question is based upon a misunderstanding.

How could these countless ages have passed, when you, the Creator of all ages, had not yet created them? What time could there have been which was not created by you? How could time pass if it had never been created? . . .

Although you are before time, you do not precede it in time. If this were so, you could not be before all time.

—*Confessions*, Books XI, XII, and XIII

The following three quotations contain a linked argument concerning time:

Does my soul tell you the truth when I say that I can measure time? I certainly measure it, but I don't know precisely what it is that I measure. I can measure the movement of bodies in time—doesn't this mean that I measure time itself? Could I measure the movement of a body—measure how long the movement lasted and how long the body took to move between two points—unless I measure the time in which it moved?

If so, how do I measure time? Do we measure longer periods by means of shorter ones, just as we measure yards by means of feet? This is how we measure the duration of a long sylla-ble—we compare it to a short one, and discover that it is twice as long. We use the same method when we measure the length of a poem by the lengths of the lines. . . .

Even so, this is not an accurate means of measuring time, because it can happen that a short line spoken slowly may take longer to re-cite than a long one spoken hurriedly. . . .

Thus it would appear to me that time is sim-ply an extension, though what it is an extension of I have no idea. I begin to wonder if it is per-haps an extension of the mind itself.

—*Confessions*, Book XI, Chap. 26

What am I measuring when I say that one period of time is longer than another, or more precisely that it is twice as long? I know I am measuring time. But I am not measuring the future, because that doesn't yet exist; nor the present, because this has no extension; nor the past, because it no longer exists. Am I measuring time which is in the process of passing but hasn't yet passed? . . .

—*Confessions*, Book XI, Chap. 26

Thus it can be said that I measure time in my own mind. I mustn't allow my mind to insist that time is something objective. I mustn't let my prejudices and preconceived notions overcome this idea. I definitely measure time in my mind. Everything that happens leaves an impression on my mind, and this impression remains long after this thing has ceased to exist. It is the impression that I measure, because it is still present, not the thing itself, which causes the impression and then disappears into the past. When I measure time it is this impression that I measure. So this is what time is—or else I don't measure time at all.

—*Confessions*, Book XI, Chap. 27

Chronology of Significant Philosophical Dates

6th C B.C.	The beginning of Western philosophy with Thales of Miletus.
End of 6th C B.C.	Death of Pythagoras.
399 B.C.	Socrates sentenced to death in Athens.
c 387 B.C.	Plato founds the Academy in Athens, the first university.
335 B.C.	Aristotle founds the Lyceum in Athens, a rival school to the Academy.

324 A.D.	Emperor Constantine moves capital of Roman Empire to Byzantium.
400 A.D.	St. Augustine writes his *Confessions*. Philosophy absorbed into Christian theology.
410 A.D.	Sack of Rome by Visigoths heralds opening of Dark Ages.
529 A.D.	Closure of Academy in Athens by Emperor Justinian marks end of Hellenic thought.
Mid-13th C	Thomas Aquinas writes his commentaries on Aristotle. Era of Scholasticism.
1453	Fall of Byzantium to Turks, end of Byzantine Empire.
1492	Columbus reaches America. Renaissance in Florence and revival of interest in Greek learning.
1543	Copernicus publishes *On the Revolution of the Celestial Orbs*, proving mathematically that the earth revolves around the sun.

1633	Galileo forced by church to recant heliocentric theory of the universe.
1641	Descartes publishes his *Meditations*, the start of modern philosophy.
1677	Death of Spinoza allows publication of his *Ethics*.
1687	Newton publishes *Principia*, introducing concept of gravity.
1689	Locke publishes *Essay Concerning Human Understanding*. Start of empiricism.
1710	Berkeley publishes *Principles of Human Knowledge*, advancing empiricism to new extremes.
1716	Death of Leibniz.
1739–1740	Hume publishes *Treatise of Human Nature*, taking empiricism to its logical limits.
1781	Kant, awakened from his "dogmatic slumbers" by Hume, publishes *Critique of Pure Reason*.

Great era of German metaphysics begins.

1807   Hegel publishes *The Phenomenology of Mind*, high point of German metaphysics.

1818   Schopenhauer publishes *The World as Will and Representation*, introducing Indian philosophy into German metaphysics.

1889   Nietzsche, having declared "God is dead," succumbs to madness in Turin.

1921   Wittgenstein publishes *Tractatus Logico-Philosophicus*, claiming the "final solution" to the problems of philosophy.

1920s   Vienna Circle propounds Logical Positivism.

1927   Heidegger publishes *Being and Time*, heralding split between analytical and Continental philosophy.

1943   Sartre publishes *Being and Nothingness*, advancing

Heidegger's thought and instigating existentialism.

1953   Posthumous publication of Wittgenstein's *Philosophical Investigations*. High era of linguistic analysis.

Chronology of St. Augustine's Life

354 A.D.	Born at Thagaste on November 13.
Early 370s	Student at Carthage. Reading Cicero ignites his interest in philosophy. He becomes attracted to Manichaeism.
382	Leaves Carthage for Rome.
Later 380s	Appointed professor at Milan. Hears Ambrose preach.
386	Conversion to Christianity.
387	Baptized by Ambrose. Returns to

	Africa (his mother Monica dies en route at Ostia).
391	Ordained as assistant priest to Valerius, Bishop of Hippo.
396	Valerius dies and Augustine succeeds him as Bishop of Hippo, the post he holds until his death.
396–411	Struggles against Donatist heretics.
399	Writes his *Confessions*.
410s	Struggles against Pelagian heretics.
413	As a consequence of fall of Rome to Visigoths, begins writing *The City of God*.
410 onward	Emigration of Pelagian heretics to North Africa.
426	Finally completes *City of God* after thirteen years, at age seventy-two.
428	Vandals invade North African provinces of Roman Empire.

430	Augustine trapped in Hippo as Vandals begin siege in May.
430	Dies on August 28 in the besieged city of Hippo, aged seventy-five.
497	Catholic bishops expelled from North Africa by Vandals take remains of Augustine with them to Sardinia.
8th century	King Luitprand of the Lombards brings Augustine's remains to Pavia in Italy.

Chronology of St. Augustine's Era

360 A.D.   Establishment of Christian community at Candida Casa in northwest Britain.

370   First appearance of migrating Black Huns in Europe, north of the Black Sea.

370 onward   Goths, displaced by westward-migrating Huns, overrun western regions of Roman Empire.

378   Visigoths defeat Romans at Adrianopole (modern-day Edirne,

	in western Turkey), destroying legend of Roman invincibility.
381	Ecumenical Council of Constantinople (present-day Istanbul).
395	Visigoths overrun Greece.
397	Death of St. Ambrose.
End of 4th century	Jewish diaspora continues, with communities now established as far afield as southern Spain and central Germany.
Early 400s	Emperor Honorius withdraws last of Roman legions from Britain.
400	Entire world population estimated at just over 250 million.
410	Rome sacked by Visigoths.
419	Death of Pelagius, leader of Pelagian heresy.
428	Vandals launch invasion of North African provinces of Roman Empire.

Middle decades of 5th century	Angles, Saxons, and Jutes begin incursions across North Sea into Britain.
430	Siege of Hippo.
431	Ecumenical Council of Ephesus.
432	End of seventy-two-year-old Christian community at Candida Casa in northwest Britain.
434	Attila the Hun, known as *Flagellum Dei* (Scourge of God), sets up headquarters in land of the Bulgars (present-day Bulgaria).

Recommended Reading

The Confessions of St. Augustine, translated by Rex Warner (New American Library, 1963)

Vernon J. Bourke, ed., *The Essential Augustine* (Hackett, 1974)

Henry Chadwick, *Augustine* (Oxford University Press, 1981)

Gerald O'Daly, *Augustine's Philosophy of Mind* (University of California Press, 1987)

Brian Stock, ed., *Augustine the Reader* (Harvard University Press, 1996)

Index

A NOTE ON THE AUTHOR

Paul Strathern has lectured in philosophy and mathematics and now lives and writes in London. A Somerset Maugham prize winner, he is also the author of books on history and travel as well as five novels. His articles have appeared in a great many publications, including the *Observer* (London) and the *Irish Times*. His own degree in philosophy was earned at Trinity College, Dublin.